DATE DUE

PRINTED IN U.S.A.

EAGLE PUBLIC LIBRARY DIST.
BOX 240 EAGLE, CO 81631
(970) 328-8800

ANIMALS UNDERGROUND
ARMADILLOS

EMILY SEBASTIAN

PowerKiDS press™

New York

Published in 2012 by The Rosen Publishing Group, Inc.
29 East 21st Street, New York, NY 10010

First Edition

Editor: Amelie von Zumbusch
Book Design: Julio Gil

Photo Credits: Cover, back cover (armadillo, fox, mongoose), pp. 4–5, 23, 24 (bottom left) Shutterstock.com; back cover (badger) Norbert Rosing/National Geographic/Getty Images; back cover (chipmunk) James Hager/Robert Harding World Imagery/Getty Images; back cover (mole) Geoff du Feu/Stone/Getty Images; pp. 7, 8–9 Theo Allofs/Photonica/Getty Images; pp. 11, 24 (top right) Danita Delimont/Gallo Images/Getty Images; p. 13 Joel Sartore/National Geographic/Getty Images; p. 15 Bianca Lavies/National Geographic/Getty Images; pp. 16–17 Joe McDonald/Visuals Unlimited/Getty Images; pp. 19, 24 (bottom right) Jeff Foott/Discovery Channel Images/Getty Images; pp. 20–21 Richard Heathcote/Getty Images; p. 24 (top left) © www.iStockphoto.com/Urban Waldenström.

Library of Congress Cataloging-in-Publication Data

Sebastian, Emily.
  Armadillos / Emily Sebastian. — 1st ed.
      p. cm. — (Animals underground)
  Includes index.
  ISBN 978-1-4488-4951-2 (library binding) — ISBN 978-1-4488-5052-5 (pbk.) —
ISBN 978-1-4488-5053-2 (6-pack)
  1. Armadillos—Juvenile literature. I. Title.
  QL737.E23S43 2012
  599.3'12—dc22
                                        2010047567
Manufactured in the United States of America

CPSIA Compliance Information: Batch #WS11PK: For Further Information contact Rosen Publishing, New York, New York at 1-800-237-9932

CONTENTS

"Armadillo" means "little armored one." Armadillos have **plates** of skin that look like armor.

Armadillos always live in warm places. This is because they get cold easily.

There are 20 kinds of armadillos. They live in North America and South America.

The armadillos in the United States are **nine-banded armadillos**. They are the state animal of Texas.

To keep themselves safe, some armadillos curl up into a ball!

An armadillo takes a big breath before it swims. This keeps it from sinking!

Armadillos dig underground **burrows**. They hide, rest, and raise their babies there.

Armadillo babies are called **pups**.
Pups drink their mothers' milk.

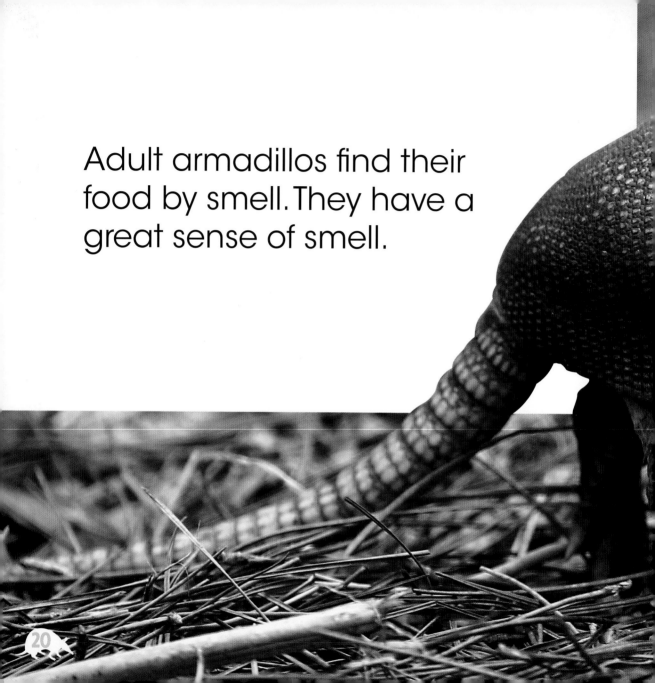

Adult armadillos find their food by smell. They have a great sense of smell.

Armadillos eat mostly bugs.
They pick up bugs with their
long tongues.

Words to Know

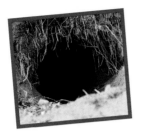

burrow

nine-banded armadillo

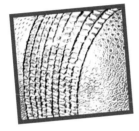

plates

pup

Index

Web Sites

Due to the changing nature of Internet links, PowerKids Press has developed an online list of Web sites related to the subject of this book. This site is updated regularly. Please use this link to access the list:
www.powerkidslinks.com/anun/armadil/